# 60 SECOND PUZZLES

HIGHLIGHTS PRESS
Honesdale, Pennsylvania

# Dozing Duck

There are at least 18 differences between these two pictures. Find as many as you can in 60 seconds and write the number you found in the "Try 1" space below. Keep trying until you find them all!

Try 1: _____ Try 2: _____

Try 3: _____ Try 4: _____

# Tic Tac Cat

The cats in each row (horizontally, vertically, and diagonally) have one thing in common. How many rows can you figure out in 60 seconds? Write the number you found in the "Try 1" space below. Keep trying until you find them all!

Try 1: _____  Try 2: _____

Try 3: _____  Try 4: _____

**Five flying felines fled fleas.**

Careless cats clawed and crawled.

**Sweetie swiftly stood to stretch and scratch.**

# Bashing Bumper Cars

What a funny mess of bumper cars! Find as many silly things as you can in 60 seconds and write the number you found in the "Try 1" space below. Keep trying until you get bumped!

Try 1: _____ Try 2: _____
Try 3: _____ Try 4: _____

# In the Jungle

Each parrot in this scene has a match. Find as many matches as you can in 60 seconds and write the number you found in the "Try 1" space below. Keep trying until you find them all!

**FLIP THE TIMER!**

There are 15 feathers hidden in this scene. How many can you find in 60 seconds?

Try 1: _____  Try 2: _____

Try 3: _____  Try 4: _____

# Fall Frenzy

From leafy yards to pumpkin patches, these fall friends need your help finding their way. Follow as many correct paths as you can in 60 seconds and write the number you finished in the "Try 1" space on the next page. Keep trying until you finish them all!

Start

Finish

Try 1: _____ Try 2: _____

Try 3: _____ Try 4: _____

**FLIP THE TIMER!**

How many words can you rhyme with fall in 60 seconds?

# Hidden Pictures®
# 6 by Six

Each of these small scenes contains 6 hidden objects from the list below. Some objects are hidden in more than one scene. Find as many as you can in 60 seconds and write the number you found in the "Try 1" space on the next page. Keep trying until you find them all!

### HIDDEN OBJECT LIST

artist's brush (3)     ring (2)
~~eraser~~ (4)     shoe ~~~~
~~~~     ~~spool~~
~~~~     tack (5)
~~~~ (2)    toothbrush (3)
~~paper clip (4)~~

**The numbers tell you how many times each identical object is hidden.**

**FLIP THE TIMER!**

Can you find which two scenes contain the exact same set of hidden objects in 60 seconds or less?

Try 1: _____ Try 2: _____

Try 3: _____ Try 4: _____

# Confident Climbers

There are at least 18 differences between these two pictures. Find as many as you can in 60 seconds and write the number you found in the "Try 1" space below. Keep trying until you find them all!

Try 1: _____ Try 2: _____

Try 3: _____ Try 4: _____

# Tic Tac Party

The piñatas in each row (horizontally, vertically, and diagonally) have one thing in common. How many rows can you figure out in 60 seconds? Write the number you found in the "Try 1" space below. Keep trying until you find them all!

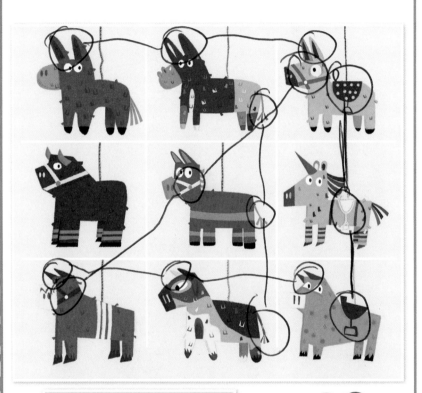

Try 1: _____ Try 2: _____

Try 3: _____ Try 4: _____

**Bertha's birthday bash broke Bailey's bat.**

Donkey drove Don down Doherty Drive.

Payton planned a parrot pasta party.

**FLIP THE TIMER!**

How many times can you say these tongue twisters correctly in 60 seconds?

# Summer Suds

This crazy car wash is getting out of hand! Find as many silly things as you can in 60 seconds and write the number you found in the "Try 1" space below. Keep trying until the cars are clean!

Try 1: _____  Try 2: _____

Try 3: _____  Try 4: _____

# Sneaky Sunglasses

Each pair of sunglasses in this scene has an exact match. Find as many matches as you can in 60 seconds and write the number you found in the "Try 1" space below. Keep trying until you find them all!

**FLIP THE TIMER!**
There are at least 18 animals in this scene. How many can you find in 60 seconds?

Try 1: _____ Try 2: _____

Try 3: _____ Try 4: _____

# Gone in 60 Seconds

These friends need your help, and they need it fast! Follow as many correct paths as you can in 60 seconds and write the number you finished in the "Try 1" space on the next page. Keep trying until you finish them all!

14

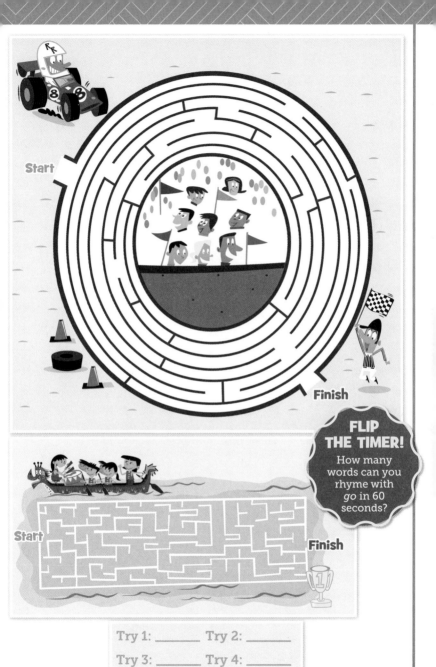

**Start**

**Finish**

**FLIP THE TIMER!**
How many words can you rhyme with *go* in 60 seconds?

**Start**

**Finish**

Try 1: _____ Try 2: _____

Try 3: _____ Try 4: _____

# Hidden Pictures®
# 6 by Six

Each of these small scenes contains 6 hidden objects from the list below. Some objects are hidden in more than one scene. Find as many as you can in 60 seconds and write the number you found in the "Try 1" space on the next page. Keep trying until you find them all!

## HIDDEN OBJECT LIST

The numbers tell you how many times each identical object is hidden.

**FLIP THE TIMER!**

Can you find which two scenes contain the exact same set of hidden objects in 60 seconds or less?

Try 1: _____  Try 2: _____

Try 3: _____  Try 4: _____

# Banana-Boat Bunch

There are at least 22 differences between these two pictures. Find as many as you can in 60 seconds and write the number you found in the "Try 1" space below. Keep trying until you find them all!

Try 1: _____ Try 2: _____
Try 3: _____ Try 4: _____

# Tic Tac Alien

The aliens in each row (horizontally, vertically, and diagonally) have one thing in common. How many rows can you figure out in 60 seconds? Write the number you found in the "Try 1" space below. Keep trying until you find them all!

Try 1: _____ Try 2: _____

Try 3: _____ Try 4: _____

**Aliens are always acting aptly.**

**Martin Martian makes mazes, maps, and matches.**

Shining stars surround Sir Sheldon sweetly.

**FLIP THE TIMER!**
How many times can you say these tongue twisters correctly in 60 seconds?

# Market Madness

It's a beautiful morning for an amusing market. Find as many silly things as you can in 60 seconds and write the number you found in the "Try 1" space below. Keep trying until the market ends!

Try 1: _____ Try 2: _____
Try 3: _____ Try 4: _____

# Pacific Pals

Many of these sea creatures have a friend who looks like them. Find as many matches as you can in 60 seconds and write the number you found in the "Try 1" space below. Keep trying until you find them all!

**FLIP THE TIMER!**

There are at least 150 bubbles in this scene. How many can you find in 60 seconds?

Try 1: _____ Try 2: _____

Try 3: _____ Try 4: _____

# Dizzying Dirt

These dutiful diggers need your help to find their way! Follow as many correct paths as you can in 60 seconds and write the number you finished in the "Try 1" space on the next page. Keep trying until you finish them all!

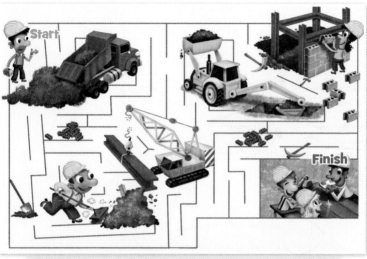

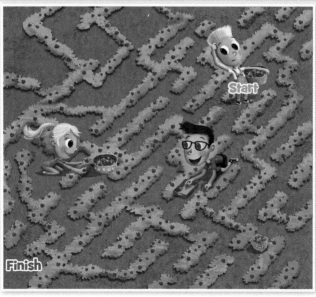

Start

Finish

Try 1: _____ Try 2: _____
Try 3: _____ Try 4: _____

Finish

Start

**FLIP THE TIMER!**

How many words can you rhyme with *mud* in 60 seconds?

23

# Hidden Pictures®
# 6 by Six

Each of these small scenes contains 6 hidden objects from the list below. Some objects are hidden in more than one scene. Find as many as you can in 60 seconds and write the number you found in the "Try 1" space on the next page. Keep trying until you find them all!

## HIDDEN OBJECT LIST

boomerang (3) ~~olive (4)~~
~~carrot~~ ~~paintbrush (4)~~
~~crescent moon (4)~~ ~~peanut (2)~~
~~ladle (2)~~ ~~ruler (4)~~
~~golf club (2)~~ ~~slice of pie (3)~~
~~mushroom (2)~~ ~~waffle (2)~~

The numbers tell you how many times each identical object is hidden.

**FLIP THE TIMER!**

Can you find which two scenes contain the exact same set of hidden objects in 60 seconds or less?

Try 1: _____   Try 2: _____

Try 3: _____   Try 4: _____

PIGS WIGS

# Super Sporty

These amazing athletes need your help to find their way. Follow as many paths as you can in 60 seconds and write the number you finished in the "Try 1" space on the next page. Keep trying until you finish them all!

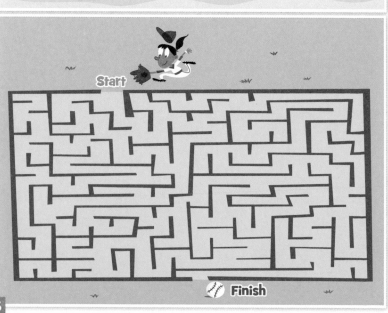

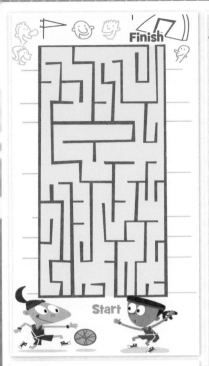

Finish

Start

Start

Finish

Try 1: _____ Try 2: _____
Try 3: _____ Try 4: _____

Start

Finish

**FLIP THE TIMER!**

How many words can you rhyme with *sport* in 60 seconds?

27

# Hidden Pictures®
# 6 by Six

Each of these small scenes contains 6 hidden objects from the list below. Some objects are hidden in more than one scene. Find as many as you can in 60 seconds and write the number you found in the "Try 1" space on the next page. Keep trying until you find them all!

### HIDDEN OBJECT LIST

banana (2)
b~~~~~ (3)
clothespin (3)
cott~~~~~
d~~~ (~~)
drumstick (4)

mitt~~~ (~~)
mu~ (2)
saucepan (2)
~~ice of~~~~~ (3)
spatu~~~
~~~~~ of orange (3)

The numbers tell you how many times each identical object is hidden.

**FLIP THE TIMER!**

Can you find which two scenes contain the exact same set of hidden objects in 60 seconds or less?

Try 1: _____ Try 2: _____

Try 3: _____ Try 4: _____

# Under-the-Sea Sillies

Everyone's enjoying time at the aquarium. Find as many silly things as you can in 60 seconds and write the number you found in the "Try 1" space below. Keep trying until the aquarium closes!

Try 1: _____ Try 2: _____
Try 3: _____ Try 4: _____

# Answers

## PAGE 2

## PAGE 3

all have a bowl → all have a toy → all have a bed →

all are sleeping →
all are stretching →
all have kittens →

all are a solid color ↗

all have a green collar ↖

## PAGE 5

## PAGE 6

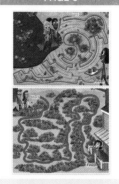

## PAGE 7

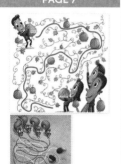

## PAGE 8

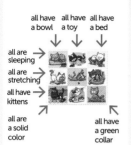

## PAGE 9

## PAGE 10

## PAGE 11

all have a blue string ↓ all have tails ↓ all have saddles ↓

all are donkeys →
all have stripes →
all are bulls →

all have bridles ↗

all have two eyes facing ↖

# Answers

## PAGE 13

## PAGE 14
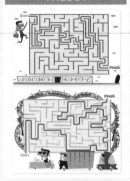

## PAGE 15
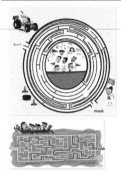

## PAGE 16

## PAGE 17

## PAGE 18
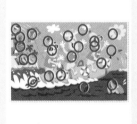

## PAGE 19

## PAGE 21

## PAGE 22